W9-CFK-391

ALL BRUGGE

Photographs: AVM, Danny de Kievith and Andrew Critchell.

Text, design, lay-out and printing completely created
by the technical department of
EDITORIAL ESCUDO DE ORO S.A.

All total or partial reproduction and
translation rights reserved.

SALE DISTRIBUTOR: Editions A.V.M. n.v.
Brugsesteenweg 93 B-8420 WENDUINE
Tel.: 050 - 42.50.72 - Fax: 050 - 42.50.74
E-mail: info@avm.be
http://www.avm.be

Editorial Escudo de Oro, S.A.

Market Square.

Market Square. Statue of Jan Breydel and Pieter de Coninck and, in the background, the 19th century Provincial Court.

INTRODUCTION

This book is designed as a lasting memento of one of the most attractive cities in the world: Brugge. Handsome patrician houses, impressive churches and exquisite works of art are the quiet testimonials of its glorious past. This past is regularly re-lived in ceremonious festivities and processions, which cannot fail to make an unforgettable impression on their spectators.

Brugge, however, is far from slumbering in the shadow of its own past. Surrounded by half a dozen active and dynamic suburban municipalities, the old town centre is like the beating heart of a living modern community. A responsible and sustained restoration programme has brought the best out of its many buildings and succeeded in filling them with new life. The sea, to which Brugge owes its origin and its blossoming period in the Middle Ages, has once more played a major role since the turn of the 20th century. Zeebrugge on the North Sea coast has developed into a harbour of worldwide stature. Visitors here will be astounded by the hum of activity peculiar to a large sea-port, and fascinated by the typical atmosphere in and around the fishing – and yacht-harbours. Numerous recreation facilities, and a pleasant safe beach afford ample opportunities for exercise, relaxation, or a beneficial rest. We may recommend you the many inviting restaurants and other eating-places with charm and atmosphere, which are to be found in Brugge and its surroundings; lovers of good food are sure to appreciate the excellent local cuisine, consisting of several expertly prepared fish and meat dishes.

Belfry or Halles Tower by night.

Market Square in the 18th century.

Baldwin erected gradually developed into a town centre, and in 875 the name of Brugge was mentioned for the first time in a chronicle.

In the course of the 10th century a trading settlement or «portus» involved in the immediate neighbourhood of the «castrum», and this contributed to the extensive growth of Brugge and Flanders. In about 1127 the various settlements became merged into one connected district, which was surrounded by canals. Charles the Good was murdered in this same year, and the tradesmen of Brugge obtained the right to participate in the administration of the town, by the election of aldermen. In this process,

FROM THEN UNTIL NOW

The destiny of Brugge has always been closely linked to the sea. A first settlement grew up, in fact, round one of the mouths which was carved out by the North Sea between the 4th and 7th centuries. In 862 Baldwin «of the Iron Arm» abducted Judith, daughter of the French King Charles the Bald. The latter found himself obliged to send his rather unwelcome son-in-law to the district of Flanders, to defend it against the increasingly aggressive Normans, who had established a «Bryggja» or mooring-place for their ships at the mouth of the Zwin. It is otherwise generally accepted that the old Norse word «Bryggja» is the origin of the present-day name of Brugge.

The citadel or «castrum» which

Rozenhoedkaai.

Brugge developed from a military fortification into a town of international importance whose power kept pace with an unhindered growth of trade.

The silting of the Zwin, Brugge's outlet to the sea, which commenced during this period, was taken in hand with the founding in 1180 of the out-port of Damme; this town was joined to Brugge by a canal.

Commerce and industry, particularly the cloth trade, made 13th century Brugge one of the most populated and prosperous cities in Europe. A smouldering feud between the powerful merchants, supported by the French king, and the less prosperous guild-members, with the Count on their

Entrance to the Beguinage in winter.

side, finally flared up in 1302 with the «Matins of Brugge» and the subsequent Battle of the Golden Spurs, in which the heir to the French throne suffered an unexpected defeat.

This struggle for power, which resulted in the guilds and trades earning a voice for themselves in the administration of the town, nevertheless did not prevent the 14th century from becoming a golden age in the history of Brugge. As a wool mart, seat of the Hanseatic towns and a world market represented by 17 nations, Brugge exercised an irresistible attraction upon merchants, bankers, and all kinds of artists.

In the same century, as a result of the marriage of Margaret van Male with Philip the Bold, the Burgundian age was ushered in, and Brugge became the centre of

Groene Rei.

a sumptuous court life. Magnificent festivities, tournaments, jousting and exquisite artistic creations were part of the expression of this pomp and splendour, yet even they could not stem the threatening tide of decay. The Zwin became silted beyond hope and Antwerp, which was now rising into the ascendancy, emerged as a rival to Brugge whose claims could not be gainsaid.

After the death of Charles the Bold and Maria of Burgundy, Brugge fell into Austrian hands, despite

A painter portrays the Groene Rei.

Groene Rei.

*The Groene Rei
in winter.*

Nightime views of the Groene Rei and the Town Square with the unmistakeable silhouette of the Belfry.

Vismarkt (Fishmarket).

Minnewater with Sluice House.

Jan van Eyck Square and one of the numerous café terraces in summer.

the valiant resistance of its inhabitants which Maximilian of Austria finally extinguished in 1488. Antwerp, meanwhile, had made capital out of this situation, and gained enormously in importance. For some time, Brugge continued to live on her former reputation, but in the 17th and 18th centuries, after the final closure of the Zwin as a trade route, she was forced to accept a minor role.

In 1794, under the French regime, Brugge became the administrative centre of the Department of

The typical tavern «De Garre».

the Leie; it was after 1815, under Dutch rule, that this district became known as West Flanders.

At the beginning of the 20th century brought a turning-point, thanks largely to the opening of the seaport of Zeebrugge in 1907. Georges Rodenbach's novel «Bruges la Morte» was one of many influences which began to attract visitors to Brugge, and these pioneers so to speak laid the foundations for Brugge as one of the most prominent touring centres of Belgium and Western Europe.

Its many monuments, buildings and works of art have miraculously survived two world wars virtually intact, and thanks also to a sensible policy of restoration Brugge is to this day an incomparable town where present and past still go harmoniously hand in hand.

A town to explore !

Carmers bridge.

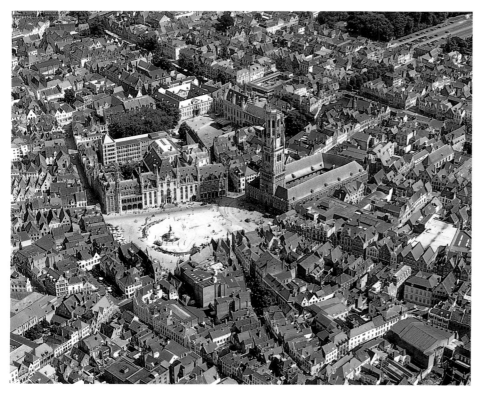

Aerial view of Market Square and the Burg.

sists of a massive copper cylinder, called a drum, which is 2.5 metres long and 2.06 metres in diameter. It is the largest in existence, weighs 9,000 kg and has 30,500 openings. Adjustable steel pins can be inserted in the openings so that in the course of rotation they come into contact with the steel staves and levers which operate the bell-clappers. The belfry keyboard is situated 19 steps higher. When playing this instrument the carilloneur sets the clappers in motion by striking the keyboard which is connected to them by a set of steel staves and levers. The belfry keyboard is played with hands and feet and requires great physical effort on the part of the carilloneur. In order to operate the

The Belfry.

A TOWN TO EXPLORE !

The best place to begin your tour of discovery is the **Market Square**, where the **Belfry** literally and figuratively sets the tone. You will experience a sense of enchantment when the 47 bronze bells start to ring out from the belfry (83 metres high). Throughout the centuries the belfry has pealed out glad tidings and messages of happy events; and some of its tidings, too, have been of sad, sombre and deathly import. The town statutes, which were announced from the balcony of the Belfry, earned the name of «Orders of the Halles». The Halles, which together form a whole with the Belfry, served for many years as a market place. In fact, every Wednesday morning the weekly market day takes place on the Market Square – a tradition dating back to the year 958.

The Belfry rewards those who climb its 366 steps, with the best views of the city. The climb also allows the carillon mechanism to be observed, made up of three parts: the bells (47 bronze bells which add up to a total of 27 tons), the keyboard and the automatic system. The celebrated «Triumphal Bell» can be seen from the 220th step, the diameter of which, is 2.05 metres, and which is only rung on very special occasions. You reach the machine room and drum after mounting the 333rd step. The belfry's automatic mechanism con-

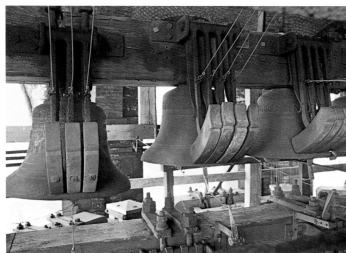

Part of the carillon mechanism.

Detail of the Belfry.

The large copper cylinder which makes the carillon work automatically.

heavier bell-clappers the player has to stamp the pedals with his feet. The **Provincial Hof** (Provincial Court) is also impressive. Until 1787 it was the Water – or Cloth-Halles; the building arches over the canal from which the flat-bottomed barges, laden to the brim with Flemish cloth, used to set off for the out-ports, to return with foreign wares of all kinds.

Most of the buildings round the Market Square have played an important role in Brugge's history. A house with a 15th century gable on the corner of the St. Amandstraat is topped with a compass-card: it is the **Boechoute House**, from which the town magistrature used to observe the festivities on the Market. Opposite stands **Craenenburg House** where Archduke Maximilian of Austria was held prisoner in 1488 when the populace rebelled against this government. Several houses on the Market Square used to belong to the

guilds, and some of them still display the symbol of their history in their architecture: the gable of the weavers' guild house is crowned with a basket, and the date 1621 shows when work began on the fishermen's guild house. And the statue in the centre of the square which represents **Jan Breydel and Pieter de Coninck** bears witness to the struggle for emancipation of the members of Brugge's guilds and crafts between 1302 and 1304. This monument was erected in their honour in 1887.

Provincial Court (19th century) and two details of Provincial Court.

Boechoute Haus and Craenenburg House.

Via the Breidelstraat you come to **the Burg** where in 864 the first county stronghold was erected as a defense against the Normans. Here the eye is rewarded with something in the nature of an architectural anthology. The lower chapel of the Basilica of the Holy Blood is in Romanesque style; the Town Hall is Gothic; the old City Clerk's Office (Griffie) is Re-

Old guild houses, with their characteristic stepped finishes, in the Market Square.

Monument to Jan Breydel and Pieter de Coninck.

naissance; the Justice Palace is classical and the Deanery (Proosdij) Baroque.

The **Town Hall** (Stadhuis), whose foundation stone was laid by Louis van Male in 1376, is one of the earliest examples of the typical building style of Brugge which has become so famous. 48 window-recesses, contained between upper and lower windows, together with the small conical towers that crown the building, accentuate a pronounced verticalism. From the balcony of the Town Hall, where the first States General of the Netherlands gathered in 1464, the Counts of Flanders used to swear their oath affirming respect of the civic liberties.

The Gothic Hall, situated on the first floor, is particularly remarkable for its magnificent wooden ceiling, carved between the end of the 14th century and beginning of the 15th century. The murals in the hall correspond to the restoration carried out at the end of the 19th century and depict historic scenes.

View of the Town Square or Burg with the Town Hall. To the left rises the Old City Clerk's Office and to the right, the Basilica of the Holy Blood.

16

Two features on the Town Hall. The figures in the niches represent famous historic persons from Brugge and the county of Flanders.

The **Old City Clerk's Office** (Oude Griffie), built in Flemish Renaissance style (1534-1537), has served in turn as the Town Clerk's Office, the Police Headquarters (after the French Revolution), as the Justice of the Peace's Office (since 1883), and finally, since 1985, as the Municipal Archives.

The **Deanery** (Proosdij), dating from 1662, where the deans of St. Donatian's Cathedral formerly exercised control and jurisdiction

Town Hall, the Gothic Room.

The Old City Clerk's Office.

over their domains, is a handsome testimonial to the Baroque style. Under the trees next to the Deanery, you can with a little imagination visualize the former majestic St. Donatian's Cathedral. This sanctuary, built in about 900, the burial place among others of Jan van Eyck and Juan Luis Vives, was demolished under the French regime in 1799; St. Saviour's Cathedral replaced it as the town's main church. On the occasion of Brugge and Salamanca being chosen European capitals of culture in 2002, the city commissioned the Japanese architect Toyo Hito with the airy Perspex and aluminium monument we see in the square today and which symbolizes the 21st century.

The **Basilica of the Holy Blood** (Basiliek van het Heilig Bloed) consists of two chapels built one over the other. The lower is the Saint Basil's Chapel, founded in 1150 by Diederik van den Elzas as the

Detail of the former Deanery. The central figure represents justice.

Monument to the 21st century, the work of Toyo Hito.

Crypt or Saint Basil's Chapel.

Basilica of the Holy Blood.

count's chapel. It was the original infrastructure of the Romanesque upper chapel, which has been re-built since the 15th century into a more spacious church in Gothic style. The relic of the Holy Blood is preserved in this upper chapel. The magnificent original stained-glass windows, destroyed during the French Revolution, were first replaced in 1845; and once again, after a bomb explosion in 1967, they were restored by the painter De Lodder of Brugge.

The Saint Basil's Chapel or Crypt has kept its original form and is the only Romanesque building of its kind in West Flanders. An incom-parable effect is achieved by the simplicity of the interior and by the stunning bareness of the walls of the three brick aisles. Throughout its splendid past the Crypt served as the Counts' chapel, the Com-panions' oratory, the Guilds' tem-ple and the Councillors' court of justice. In this chapel is preserved the beautiful 14th century mas-

terpiece of Our Lady of Charity, also known as the Pietà. The Ecce Homo statue can also be seen here: a great work of art and an unrivalled piece of wood-carving. Behind a cast-iron grille you may glimpse part of the original small round tiles of the authentic floor-work.

The upper chapel is a treasury of works of art: paintings, carvings, the work of gold – and silversmiths, a marble altar, and a wooden pul-pit in the form of a terrestrial globe,

Pietà and Ecce Homo (crypt).

Main altar to the upper chapel.

The Last Supper, the 16th century alabaster work which decorates the main altar table.

sculpted in the 18th century by H. Pulincx. The great attraction in the museum of the basilica is undoubtedly the reliquary shrine, the work of Jan Crabbe (17th century), executed in gold and silver, and decorated with precious stones.

According the tradition, the relic of the Holy Blood was brought to Brugge as the time of the Second Crusade, having been venerated in Constantinople. Every year in May, on Ascension Day, the Procession of the Holy Blood files through the decorated streets of the town. It is Brugge's most important folkloric event. More than two thousand people take part in this colossal pageant. The differ-

Altar of the Precious Blood.

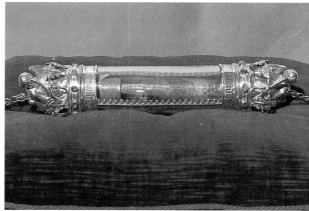

The relic of the Holy Blood.

Shrine of the Holy Blood.

Stained-glass windows Basilica.

Procession of the Holy Blood.

BRUGGES SCHOONSTE DAG

View of Blinde Ezelstraat (Blind Donkey street), with the archway of the Old City Clerk's Office.

Huidenvettersplaats and detail of the column whose emblem is connected with the cobbler's trade.

ent groups which escort the relic, adorned according to the old customs evoke of Brugge during its times of splendour, under the Burgundies.

Going down **Blinde Ezelstraat** (Blind Donkey street), the name of which comes from a lodging house that was once here, leads to the **Fish Market** (Vismarkt) and the **Huidenvettersplaats** or the **Tanner's square.** The 17th century house at number 10 was the former headquarters of the Tanner's Guild, the importance of which gave rise to this square's central column. Next we come to the **Rosary Wharf** (Rozenhoedkaai), a picturesque corner which is sure to arouse your romantic imagination. The lofty spire of Our Lady's Church is already visible in the distance.

Halfway along the wharf is the **Saint Jans Nepomucenusbrug Bridge** with a statue dedicated to this saint from Brugge, who was the Archbishop of Prague. In 1393 he was made a martyr, having refused to betray the secrets of the con-

*Saint Jans
Nepomucenus-
brug Bridge.*

Saint Jans Nepomucenusbrug Bridge and Wollestraat. At the bottom of which the Belfry can be seen.

fession, and later thrown into the waters of the river Moldau.

Stroll along the **Dijver** past the buildings of the **College of Europe**, and turn in left to the **Groeninge Museum**. This Municipal Museum of Fine Arts, built in the grounds of the old Eeckhout Abbey, contains an exceptionally rich collection of paintings by the socalled Flemish Primitives. Among the works on view here are masterpieces by Jan van Eyck, Rogier van der Weyden, Gerard David, Hugo van der Goes and Hans Memling. Also represented are the

most important artistic trends up to the present time. The «Imaginary Van Eyck Museum» is a splendid addition to what can be seen here: a room in which a collection of remarkably well produced colour slides of different sizes is displayed gives an excellent panorama of the work of this great Flemish painter.

Turning left as you leave the museum, you enter a peaceful green oasis in the heart of the town, namely the **Arents Court** (Hof Arents). Here you will find the **Arentshuis**, which is also a mu-

The river Dijver and Saint Jans Nepomucenusbrug Bridge.

Groeninge Museum. «The Baptism of Christ», by Gerard David († 1523). Photographic archive, Groeninge Museum. Photographer: M. Platteeuw, Brugge.

Groeninge Museum. «The Moreel Triptych» (1484), by Hans Memling († 1494). Photographic archive, Groeninge Museum. Photographer: M. Platteeuw, Brugge.

Groeninge Museum. «The Virgin and the canon», by Jan van Eyck († 1441). Photographic archive, Groeninge Museum. Photographer: M. Platteeuw, Brugge.

Groeninge Museum. «The tithing» (detail), by Pieter Bruegel jr. (1564-1638). Photographic archive, Groeninge Museum. Photographer: M. Platteeuw, Brugge.

Saint Bonifacius bridge.

seum, housing three different collections: etchings and watercolours which the English artist Frank Brangwyn bequeathed to his native city Brugge, a valuable collection of porcelain, pewter and earthenware, donated to the town by Miss Herssens of Hamme/Sint-Niklaas, in 1977, and finally a series of remarkable oil-paintings of the town in former times.

The quaint little **Bonifacius Bridge** and the bust of the Spanish humanist Juan Luis Vives meet you on your way to the inner courtyard of the **Gruuthuse Palace**.

The Lords of Gruuthuse, who once lived in this palace, had the sole right of sale of the «gruut», a blend of dried plants used in the spicing of beer. One of the most famous scions of this family was certainly Louis van Gruuthuse, who proclaimed the motto «Plus est en Vous» in his coat of arms. He was a capable diplomat, politician and warrior in the service of the Dukes of Burgundy. During his extremely active life he organized, among other things, many tournaments, extended a generous refuge to the exiled English King Edward IV

(1471), and amassed an outstanding collection of books and miniatures which can still be admired in the Bibliotheque Nationale in Paris.

The palace now serves as a museum, where a most varied patrimony is on exhibition: lace, coins, tapestries, musical instruments, weapons, furniture, kitchen equipment and so on.

There is also a **stone museum** with tombstones and archaeological findings on display.

The entire group of buildings is dominated by the spire of **Our Lady's Church** (Onze-Lieve-Vrou-

Gruuthuse Palace.

Courtyard of Gruuthuse Museum.

Typical upper part of the entrance to the Gruuthuse Museum, seen from the inner courtyard.

Gruuthuse Museum main façade: mounted statue of Louis van Gruuthuse.

wekerk), which ranks in majesty with the tower of the Belfry.
Of Gothic styling and a Latin cross layout with five aisles, construction work began on the church in 1210. The tower, 122 metres in height, was finished in 1549.
The Madonna and Child by Michelangelo, sculpted in white marble, is one of the gems of the unusually rich art collection belonging to the church. It is also one

Gruuthuse Museum. General view of the kitchen.

37

Church of Our Lady.

Saint Bonifacius bridge and Church of Our Lady.

of the rare works by this great artist which can be viewed outside Italy. Also of exceptional interest are the splendid monumental tombs of Maria of Burgundy and Charles the Bold; the prayer tribune of the Lords of Gruuthuse; and the choir with the coats of arms of the knights who attended the 11th chapter of the Golden Fleece here in 1468.

The **Saint John's Hospital** (Sint-Janshospital) stands in the shadow

The apse in the Church of our Lady.

Church of Our Lady. Main altar and organ.

Church of Our Lady. Madonna and the Child, white marble statuette (1503-1504) by Michelangelo.

Church of Our Lady. Mausoleums of Mary of Burgundy and Charles the Bold.

Church of Our Lady. Tomb with frescoes.

Saint John's Hospital. On the right, the entrance of the Memling Museum.

of Our Lady's Church. Since the second half of the 12th century it has served not only as a hospital, but also as a lodging for travellers. Constructed in the 12th century, it was used up until 1977, making it one of the oldest working hospitals in Europe.

Saint John's Hospital. Detail of the typanum on the church façade in which the Virgin Mary's is depicted whilst sleeping and during her Coronation.

Saint John's Hospital. Inner courtyard.

Until 1634 the hospital was run by two orders of monks and nuns. The nuns continued to carry out their duties until 1977, when the hospital was transferred to a modern building on the outskirts of the town. Victims of the plagues in times of epidemic were taken into the lower rooms along the water's edge. The hospital's old pharmacy is a very realistic museum in which the ceramic and metal mixing-vessels used in olden times have been carefully pre-

Saint John's Hospital seen from the canal.

«The Virgin Mary with the Apple», by Hans Memling.

«The Mystical Marriage of Saint Catherine» (detail), by Hans Memling.

served and stored in beautifully carved wooden cupboards.

Within the hospital, in one of the large patients wards, is the **Memling Museum**, with a collection of some of the most delicate and perfect works by Hans Memling (1433-1494) The jewel of the collection is the big triptych «The Mystical Marriage of Saint Catherine»; the portraits of «Sybilla Sambetha»

and «Martin van Nieuwenhove», the «Pieta», «The Adoration of the Magi» and the «Saint Ursula Shrine» have also enraptured countless visitors. They are the works of a truly refined spirit which has penetrated into the deepest secrets of the art of painting.

Hans Memling, who was of German origin, after spending periods in Cologne and Brussels, settled de-

finitively in Brugge, where he became a Free Master of Saint Luke's Guild in 1467. A rather more poetic though not altogether verifiable account of his life tells how he was wounded at the Battle of Nancy while serving Charles the Bold as a mercenary soldier. According to this legend, he bequeathed a number of his masterpieces to the Saint John's Hospital in

Shrine of Saint Ursula. Episodes in the saint's life are depicted in this miniature masterpiece painted by Hans Memling in 1489. The wooden display case is in the shape of a gothic chapel.

45

«Walplaats» with spire of Church of Our Lady.

recognition of the good treatment he received there.

Do not leave the Saint John's Hospital without visiting the Old Apothecary, the Guardian's Room and the Convent Chapel.

As you cross the **Maria Bridge**, you will notice one of the many «godshuizen» or almshouses which are a characteristic feature of the town: in this case, the «Rooms Couvent». These institutions were placed by wealthy families or trade associations of Brugge at the disposal of the aged and needy.

Turning right through the narrow Stoofstraat and crossing the **Walplaats**, where in sunny weather you can watch the **lacemakers** deftly plying their bobbins, you come to the **Beguinage** (Begijnhof). This is virtually a miniature town within a town, where time seems to have stood still. In 1299, approximately a century and a half after its foundation, it was raised by Philip the Fair to the stature of a Princely Beguinage, and thus ceased to come under the jurisdiction of the town. The Beguinage

Detail of the «Walplaats».

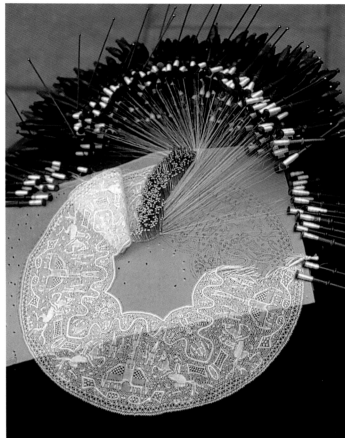

Lacemaker of Brugge.

developed with the entry into it of girls from all social backgrounds who dedicated themselves to a mystical community life, under the leading of a superintendent called the Grand Mistress. But the history of the Beguinage has not always presented a rosy picture: it was ravaged in turn by flood, fire, iconoclasm and the French Revolution. The place of the beguines, who belong to the past as

Lace making. The finest or most elaborate is that which is made in «Brugge stitch» in which there are more than 300 bobbins.

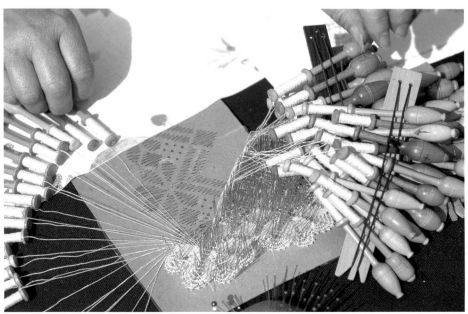

Bridge and entrance to the Beguinage.

far as Brugge is concerned, has been taken by the Benedictine Sisters, who still wear a garb reminiscent of the 15th century inhabitants of the cloister. You can get a good idea of the former lifestyle of the beguines by visiting the typical little house next to the entrance.

In the close neighbourhood of the Beguinage lies the romantic **Minnewater lake**. It is difficult nowadays to imagine the hum of

Beguinal church consecrated to Saint Elizabeth.

The Beguinage is one of the quietest and most beautiful places in Brugge.

A carriage ride by the side of the Minnewater.

activity connected with the load
ing and unloading of the many
vessels which used to drop ancho
here. Swans now glide noiselessly
over the water, like white-rigged
sailing-boats to whom shipwreck
is unknown.
Retracing your steps along the
Wijngaard street, by Katelijnestraa
where at number 43 is the **Brugge**
Diamond Museum (Diamantmu
seum Brugge). The technique fo
polishing diamonds by means o

Minnewater.

Swans on the Minnewater.

Minnewater. Churchspire of Our Lady in the background.

51

Brugge Diamond Museum: a reacreation of the Lodewijk van Barquem workshop.

The Brugge Diamond Museum organises daily demonstrations of how these precious stones are cut and polished.

a rotating disk was invented in Bruges in the 15th century by the goldsmith, Lodewijk van Berquem. The rich dukes of Burgundy promoted the expansion of the jewellery and diamond industry and many European monarchs came to own jewels made in the workshops of Brugge. This museum reveals the history of the diamond industry both in Brugge and the country, as well as the legendary inventor's workshop, the chance to see a demonstration of how the diamonds are cut and to admire a varied display of diamond jewellery.

From Katelijnestraat, by H.-Geeststraat you reach the **Saint Saviour's Cathedral** (Sint-Salvatorskathe-draal). This building has slowly evolved since the 9th century into a Gothic whole such as it is today (with the exception of the Romanesque base of the tower, which dates from about 1200) and prides itself on being the oldest brick building in Belgium. Having suffered as many as four fires and also having survived the upheaval of the French Revolution. This sanctuary was raised to the stature of a cathedral in 1834.

Inside the church, the visitor's eye is immediately drawn to the magnificent pulpit constructed by H. Pulincx jr. in 1785, and to the technically and artistically splendid organ which has provided pleasure for countless music lovers.

Examples of diamonds without settings and set in a ring.

Saint Saviour's Cathedral.

Saint Saviour's Cathedral.
Main choir.

Various trades, such as the cobblers and coachmakers, had their own chapels within this sanctuary. As in the Church of Our Lady, the Order of the Golden Fleece held one of its chapters here in 1478. The small carved wooden figures on and under the arm-rests of the choir, which was constructed to

Saint Saviour's Cathedral. Organ loft and organ; to the left in the picture, the barroque pulpit can be seen, the work of H. Pulincx. Jr. Early 18th century bronze door under the organ loft.

Saint Saviour's Cathedral. Choir and stained-glass window.

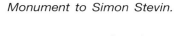
Monument to Simon Stevin.

SIMON STEVIN.

commemorate the above chapter, are individual works of art.

The church's art patrimony consists further of several remarkable paintings, the majestic high altar flanked by two late Baroque monumental tombs of former bishops of Brugge, and a number of valuable tapestries. Equally outstanding is a sculpture of the Creator, of somewhat grand dimensions, the work of Artus Quellin from 1682. The adjoining museum contains in addition to paintings by Dirk Bouts, Pieter Pourbus and Adriaan Isenbrant a considerable amount of precious gold and silverwork, sculpture and embroidery.

Notice, too, as you leave the cathe-dral the little passion-house where a dramatic Christ figure is seen kneeling in front of the cross.

Entering the **Steenstraat**, keen shoppers are sure to feel their hearts beating a little faster. Together with the **Noordzandstraat** which runs parallel to it, this street is undeniably one of the shopping paradises of Brugge. The choice of goods in the shops, ranging from sophisticated boutiques to well-stocked supermarkets, is appealing to every taste. Proof of the fact that trading establishments are not merely interested in profit is the very successful restoration of a pair of gabled store-fronts

Views of the 't Zand and the new Concert Hall.

carried out largely at the owners' own cost.

Next to Steenstraat is the **Simon Stevin square**, presided over by a statue of this illustrious learned Dutch man born in Brugge (1548-1620). It is here where every year, the **Christmas Market** is held.

From here we can continue on to the Market Place, or make a detour to visit two pleasant squares. One is the **'t Zand** esplanade, at the end of Zuidzandstraat, to the west of Steenstraat, presided over by a great fountain, the work of sculptures Depuydt-Canestrano. The fountain is decorated with various sculptured groups: the female figures symbolising the four great Flemish cities, (Antwerp, Ghent, Courtrai and Brugge), the fisherman and his companions make reference to the age-old link between Brugge and the sea, also evocative are the polders or «Netherlands» by Jacques Brel, and above the cyclists the legendary heroes Tyl Ulenspiegel (the mischievous prankster Tyl) and his girlfriend Nele. In the 't Zand is placed the Tourism Office and nearby is the new Concert Hall.

The other square is **Muntplein,** accessed from 't Zand by the streets Geldmunt and Geerwinstraat. Here we can admire the equestrian statue of Maria, the duchess of Burgundy and sovereign of Flanders, who died at a young age as the result of falling off her horse whilst hunting. Her body lies in Our Lady's Church.

In the meantime we have made our way back to the Market, where

Monument to Maria, the Duchess of Burgundy and the sovereign of Flanders.

Municipal Theatre.

a delicious cup of coffee or a frothing pint of beer make a nice way to round off a preliminary acquaintance with the old town of Brugge.

If this first reconnaissance of Brugge has whetted your appetite, you will find the Market Square a good starting-point for a second tour of exploration. The **Vlamingstraat**, where various financial institutions are no accidental reminder of the economic activity which characterized this district, leads you straight into the old «Hanseatic Brugge».

Near the Vlamingstraat, the square now occupied by the **Municipal Theatre** (Stadsschouwburg) housed for a number of years (1468-1478) the «Platform of Liège» (Luikse Perron), a freedom symbol of that fiery town which was transferred here by Charles the Bold as a punishment to the rebellious inhabitants of Liège. In front of the Municipal Theatre, the construction of which was completed in 1869, is a statue by the local sculpture Jef Claerhout which represents Papageno, the protagonist of Mozart's «Magic Flute«.

On the right of the theatre stands the **Nation House of Genoa**. Two other Italian Nation Houses, those of Florence and Venice used to be situated in the immediate neighbourhood. Nowadays it houses a restaurant and a bookshop. Merchants gathered here, stored their wares here and established their consulates on this spot. Although Brugge cannot lay claim to a stock exchange, or bourse, she was instrumental in the origin of the name: in front of the **Huis Ter Beurze**, which was once the home of the Van der Beurze family, merchants used to carry out all kinds of business such as the exchange of money and so forth, in just the

Spiegelrei with former Porters' Lodge in the background.

same way as this is still done in the established stock exchanges of the world's major cities.

The **Academiestraat**, embellished by various attractive Renaissance gables, leads you into a square dominated by the statue of Jan van Eyck and surrounded by impressive buildings.

The **Porter's Lodge** was a gathering-place and relaxation centre for prominent porters. The name «porter» did not refer to someone living within the city gates, though it originates from the term «portus». In a niche of the building, which serves at present as the Royal Archives, the «Little Bear of Brugge» proudly stands. During certain festivities it is often dressed up in different costumes. The bear, which also appears in the town's coat-of-arms, seems to have been the first living creature that Baldwin of the Iron Arm met in this hitherto inhospitable terrain about 11 centuries ago.

The **Old Toll House**, later converted into the Local Library and nowadays the Local Information Centre, the **Pijndershuis** next door to it are another reminder of the busy trade which was once carried on here. The Lords of Luxembourg used to exact a toll on the ship's cargoes which passed through the hands of the «pijnders» or dockers.

A memorial tablet on **De Rode Steen**, a corner-house on the left of the **Spiegelrei,** commemorates Georges Rodenbach, the author of the famous novel «Bruges la Morte».

The **Genthof**, where the wooden gables have gradually disappeared since the 18th century on account of fire-risk, and the **Wednesday Market** (Woensdagmarkt) with its statue of Hans Memling, are passed on the way

The Porters' House.

to the **Oosterlingenplaats**. It was here that the powerful members of the German Hanseatic League from Cologne, Lubeck, Hamburg and other cities established their business houses. They contributed largely to the important role played by Brugge –together with London, Bergen and Novgorod– as a Hanseatic centre.

From the **Spaanse Loskaai**, where the **Nation House of Castile** among others was situated, you cross the **Augustines' Bridge** (1391) and turn left to the **Vlaming Bridge**. A handsomely restored brick oriel window, commissioned by the goldsmiths' guild and originally used as a smelting-furnace for gold, will attract your attention here. Across the bridge and righthanded through the Pieter Pourbusstraat, you now make your way to **Saint James's Church** (St-Jakobskerk).

This church, dating from 1240, came into its own in the 15th century thanks to generous gifts from the Dukes of Burgundy and foreign merchants. It was, however, yet another victim of the vandalism of the Iconoclasts (1580). Spectacular restoration work was carried out in the following two centuries, mainly in Baroque style.

It is only possible to give a short summary of the many art treasures on view here: the brass burial tablet of Catherine D'Ault; the monumental tomb of Ferry de Gros (treasurer of the Golden Fleece); an enamelled terra-cotta (Madonna and Child) by Della Robbia; and noteworthy paintings by J. van Oost, A. Cornelis and L. Blondeel.

Along the St. Jacobstraat in the

The Kruispoort.

direction of the Market, you may turn left into the Naaldenstraat. The **Bladelin Court**, originally the home of Peter Bladelin –treasurer of the Golden Fleece and the Duke of Burgundy's chamberlain– came into the possession of the Medici family in 1466. Tomasso Portinari, Lorenzo de Medici's banking agent, took up his residence here and finally acquired possession of the building in 1480. A number of medallions in the courtyard walls

The Kruispoort entrance from the canal.

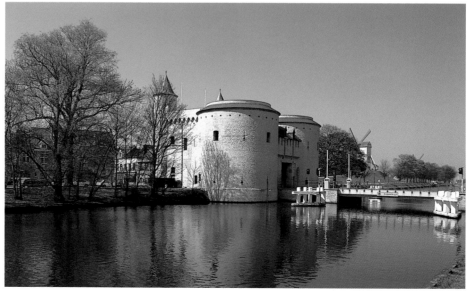

The Ezelpoort.

The Smedenpoort.

62

portray some of its most famous inhabitants.

At the end of this street, turning right through the Kuipersstraat, you reach the **Eiermarkt**, where several colourful cafe terraces, in summer at least, invite you to take a breather. Here you meet once more the Bear of Brugge, proudly sculpted on top of the artistic stone pump which is a feature of this little square.

A good place to begin a tour of folkloric Brugge is the **Kruispoort**. You can reach it on foot from the Market via the Breidelstraat, Hoogstraat and Langestraat. Frequent bus services will drop you off there in a matter of moments.

Where the present Kruispoort now stands there were once two fortifications. Traces of their junction are still visible on the city walls which have since disappeared. The building houses a museum providing a survey of over a century

Windmill on the Kruispoort rampart.

Monument to Guido Gezelle.

and a half of military history, the main accent being placed on the two world wars.

In addition to the Kruispoort, three other city gates –namely the **Gentpoort**, **Ezelpoort** and **Smedenpoort**– have been preserved almost intact. The remainder were systematically demolished under the rule of Emperor Joseph II in the 18th century. A bronze skull has been inserted in one of the walls of the Smedenpoort, to commemorate the treachery of an inhabitant of Eeklo, who attempted to open the city gates to the occupier in 1691.

Not far from the Kruispoort, the air is cleft by the sails of **three windmills**. One of them, the **St.-Janshuismolen**, is still in active service and can be visited and seen in full operation during the summer months. Marcus Gerards' plan, drawn in 1562, shows 25 mills on the ramparts, where the wind is caught to best advantage. On the left of the first mill, in the Rolweg, stands the birthplace of Brugge's famous poet **Guido Gezelle** (1830-1899). Purchased by the Town Council in 1925, it is today a literary and didactic museum where the poet's life and work are on view. Several street names in this part of town bear witness to Gezelle's contemporaries such as Hugo Verriest, Albrecht Rodenbach and Stijn Streuvels.

You will also discover in the Rolweg the grounds and buildings of the **Crossbow Archers' Guild of Saint George**. One street further. in the Carmersstraat, is situated the building complex of the **Saint Sebastian's Guild**. Like their comrades-

Birthplace of Guido Gezelle.

Museum of Folklore.

in-arms of the Saint George's Guild, this association's longbow archers formed part of the town militia in the middle ages. The emblem of Jerusalem in their coat of arms indicates that they also took part in the crusades.

Further down the Carmersstraat is the **English Convent**, where Guido Gezelle spent his last days.

Turning left through the Korte Speelmansstraat you enter the Balstraat. A row of little houses, in which retired members of the cobblers' guild used to be lodged, has been restored and converted

Museum of Folklore. Old tavern.

65

into the **Museum of Folklore**. Old-fashioned interiors have been tastefully reconstructed to include, among others, a sitting-room, an inn, a herbalist's shop and a pharmacy.

Across the street the **Lace Centre** (Kantcentrum) goes to great lenghts to keep up the centuries' old tradition of bobbin lacemaking, as well as adding a modern flavour to the classical designs. Here, regular courses and so-called «open lace days» are provided for enthusiasts who wish to master the deft art of manipulating lace bobbins.

The **Jerusalem Church** (Jerusalemkerk) towers above both these groups of buildings. It is quite remarkable for its unique blend of highly diverse building styles. The church, which has a Gothic substructure crowned by a bell-tower of oriental appearance, was built on the commission of the noble Italian Adornes family, who settled in Brugge in the 13th century. The plans for the church were based on those of the old Church of the Holy Sepulchre in Jerusalem, where various members of the Adornes family went on pilgrimage.

When visiting this church, make a point of studying the magnificent stained-glass windows (1482), which are the oldest in Brugge; the monumental grave of Anselm Adornes and his wife; the white stone altar and calvary; and the crypt and Holy Sepulchre, which in conception and size is a faithful copy of the Holy Sepulchre in Jerusalem. Next to the church there remain to this day six of the original twelve «godshuizen» for

The Vlissinghe inn, the oldest in the city, still working.

Saint Giles's Church.

poor widows built by the Adornes family.

In the close vicinity, the spire of **Saint Anna's Church** (Sint-Anna-kerk) points towards the sky. This place of worship, where Guido Gezelle among others was baptized, has often been appropriately described as a «drawing-room church». Having been destroyed by the Beggar Protestants (Geuzen) in 1581, it was rebuilt, thanks to generous subscriptions by art-loving families, into a harmonious whole in which marble, copper, woodcarving and vaulting arches mutually complete one another.

In the Blekersstraat, a sidestreet of the Jeruzalemstraat, is to be found the oldest tavern in the town, namely the **Vlissinghe**. In its old-fashioned 16th – 17th century interior you can pick up strength before resuming the last part of your walk.

The Blekersstraat runs into the St. Annarei; turning right and crossing the second bridge, through the St. Gilliskoorstraat, a sidestreet of the Lange Rei, you approach **Saint Giles's Church** (Sint-Gilliskerk). It is an eloquent example of what is technically known as a «hall church» (three aisles of equal height). Famous painters such as Hans Memling, Lancelot Blondeel and Pieter Pourbus are thought to be buried either in the church or in the adjacent churchyard.

Back to the Lange Rei and over the next bridge, the Potterierei beckons to you. The imposing buildings of the **Episcopal Seminary** stand in the place once occupied by the Abbey of the Dunes, origi-

Potterierei. «The Seven Plaguehouses».

nally founded in Koksijde, and whence the last Cistercians were expelled by the French regime in 1796. Several works of art are housed in the Seminary, including a noteworthy collection of miniatures which unfortunately are not on view to the public.

Our Lady of the Potterie is a hospice founded in 1276, where old people are still taken care of. The buildings consist of a chapel and a museum with an incredible wealth of art treasures, including gold and silver chalices, monstrances,

Potterie Church.

censers, etc. The name «Potterie» commemorates the potters who had their chapel here.

This sanctuary once provided shelter for unfortunate women. The image of Our Lady of the Potters' Guild above the altar can be admired to this day: it has been venerated since the 13th century. Every year, on the eve of the Assumption of Our Lady the procession of Our Lady of the Blind sets forth from the neighbourhood of Brugge to light a candle here in devotion to Our Lady. This tradition originated during the wars of the 14th century, when Our Lady took the inhabitants of Brugge under her protection.

From the Lange Rei you can conclude your exploration with a busride back to the Market. Otherwise you may return along the Potterierei and the St. Annarei as far as the Blekersstraat, turn right over the bridge and take the second street to the left, which brings you to **Saint Walburga's Church**.

This church, consecrated to Saint Francis Xavier, has undergone the same turbulent history as the Jesuit order which vouched for its construction. After the abolition of the Order in 1779, it was granted the role of a parish church. During the French Revolution the church went through hard times, and was converted into a Temple of Reason. Notwithstanding its restless past, the church still harbours numerous pieces which are a testimony to its earlier glory: the pulpit sculpted by Quellinus the Younger, the communion rail, the magnificent choir, the statues of the apostles, etc.

Saint Walburga's Church.

69

One of the most appealing ways to get to know Brugge is by taking a boat trip on its canals, highly recommended equally by day as by night.

A ride in the traditional horse and carriage is also a pleasant way to tour Brugge.

Damme. Town Hall.

DAMME

The Flemish landscape round Brugge is distinctly beautiful. In a varied countryside of woods, water, polders and farmland, midst quiet villages, castles and typical farms, is the setting of the town of Damme, just a few kilometres from Brugge, by the side of the Brugge-Sluis canal. Originally the town was situated on a dam, from where its name was derived, and gained great prosperity during the middle Ages as a result of its construction in 1180, just before the port of Brugge, due to the progressive aridness of the river Zwin. But from the beginning of the 16th century, the importance gained by the port of Antwerp and the definitive closure of the Zwin as a river route, brought about its decline as a great commercial centre.

Some of the buildings are testimony to its illustrious past, such as the Town Hall, Saint John's Hospital and Our Lady's church. The **Town Hall**, constructed between 1464 and 1467, presents on its principal façade an arched terrace with two flights of steps flanked by lions. The statues in the niches represent important people from Flanders and Burgundy, such as Philip of Alsace, Charles the Bold, and the statue in front of the Town Hall is that of Jakob van Maerlant, the 13th century writer who for the first time wrote his literary work in Dutch, for which he is considered to be the father of Dutch poetry. Inside the Town Hall is the museum of the town's history. The **Saint John's Hospital**

Damme. Church of Our Lady.

was founded by Margaret of Constantinople in the 13th century and now houses a museum with furniture, documents and art works from bye-gone times. **Our Lady's church** was also built in the 13th century. With its impressive tower all of 45 metres in height, which it is recommended to climb to enjoy unforgettable views of Damme and its surroundings.

Another point of interest is the **Ulenspiegel Museum**, dedicated to this popular hero who fought for Belgium's liberty against the foreign ruler, king Philip of Austria. According to tradition, Tyl Ulenspiegel (Tyl the mischievous prankster) was born in Damme in 1527. The museum is housed in the so called De grotte Sterre, in a 15th century brick built house, the oldest in the city, situated opposite the Town Hall.

Along the canal, the visitor will also be delighted by the charm of the windmill, an old farmhouse and the typical lines of trees.

Damme. Windmill.

Damme. The tree lined banks of the Brugge-Sluis canal.